Beach Beauties

Fashion Sketchbook Collection

Adult Coloring books by S. Parks

VOLUME II

Reviews are always welcome. With this issue, I've named the models so that you can share your favorites in your reviews. Enjoy!

Cover and Interior Art by
Stephen A Parks ©2016

Thank you for buying this second edition of Fashion Sketchbook series; a coloring book collection of hand-drawn illustrations by Stephen A Parks.

Discover the full collection:
- Elven Beauties
- Beach Beauties
- Christmas Beauties {Coming December 2016}

Thanks to Jennifer for doing the final outlines.

GUINN

Rachel

AYUUKO

FARAH

Acacia

Sasha

Karra and Ty

Ren

Sade

Prisilla

JOSELYNN

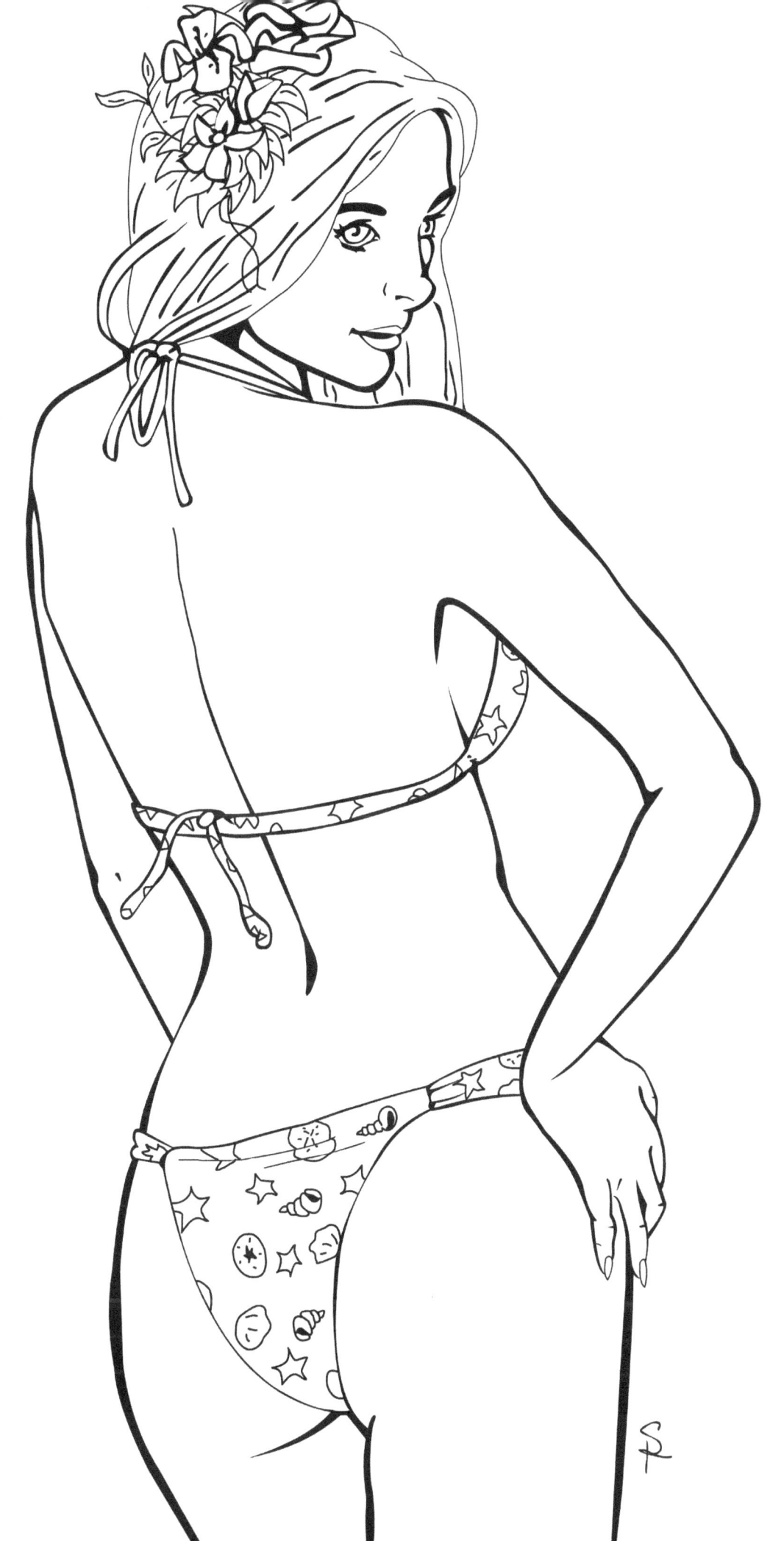

Jenni

Penelope

Wendy

ALANI

LAYLA

Jenna

Lexi

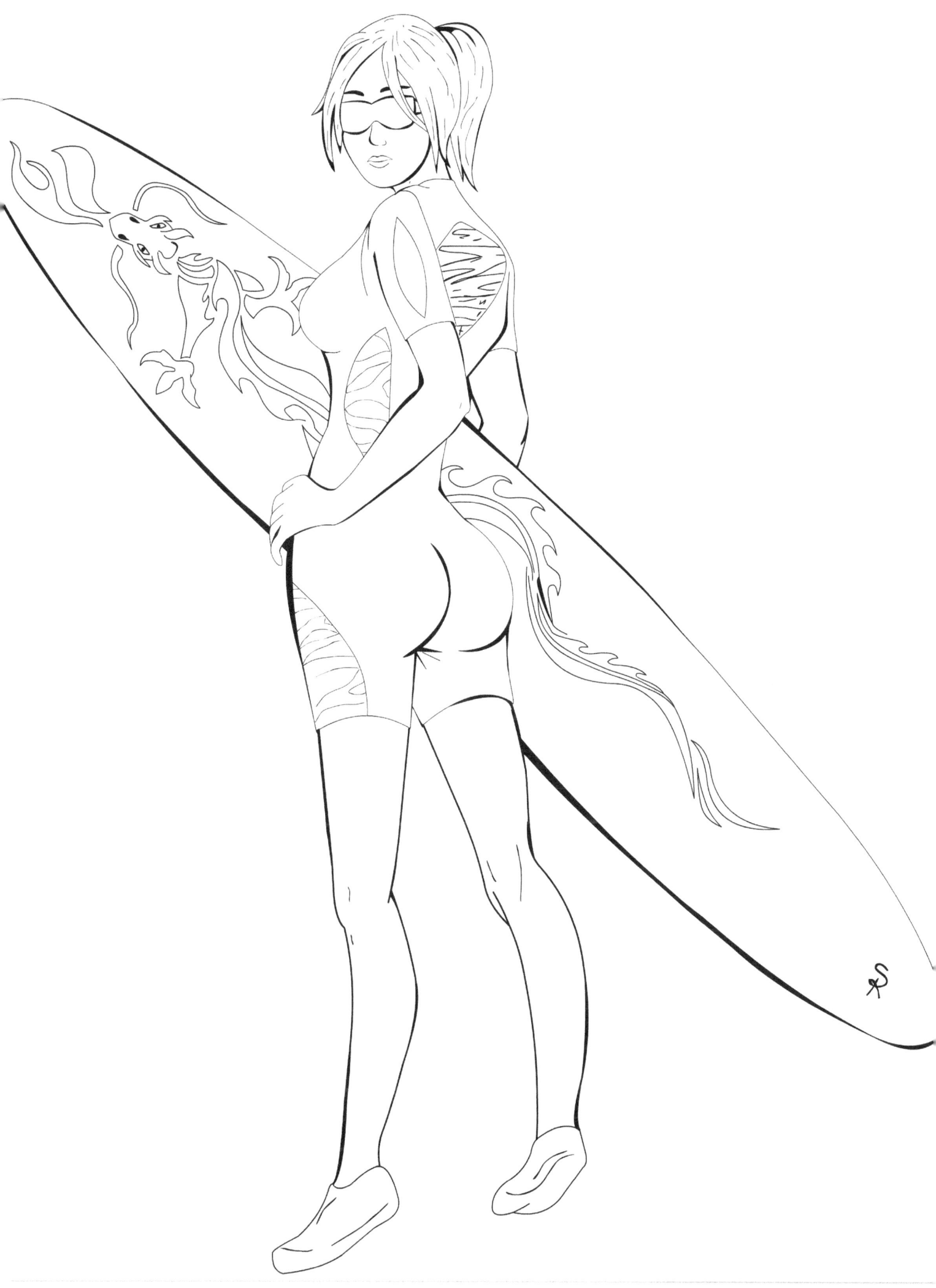

Anabel

Janicka

Reanna and Ferris

DJAMILA

TAMARA

Thank you!
Look forward to my next book; Christmas Beauties, coming December 2016

www.ingramcontent.com/pod-product-compliance
Lightning Source LLC
Chambersburg PA
CBHW080556190526
45169CB00007B/2795